MI
SE
MARR AGE

CW01604295

Mindfulness, the chance to choose.

By Leigh Eastman

'You have to keep going to get anywhere' is a favourite Mantra of mine. What is the alternative? Every journey begins with one single step, this could be your first step to the incredible, amazing, exciting life you were born to live x

FSC

Copyright © Leigh Eastman 2014
The Author asserts the moral right to be identified as the originator of this work.

ISBN 978 0 9929690 2 8

Published by Leigh Eastman

About the author

Leigh Eastman has been a successful therapist for over 17 years. During that time she has qualified in 14 complementary therapies. Her greatest passions to date are teaching Pilates and doing massage. She also runs Mindfulness Workshops. She works out of Eden Therapy Centre in Hampshire with her son who is an Osteopath and also a Pilates instructor. Her daughter lives in London and works for the BBC.

Leigh believes that you can create anything you want in your life. She believes you can be who you want to be, have what you want to have but most importantly you can find peace no matter what.

Foreword by Leigh

I first decided to write a book about relationships because of what I had learned and experienced over the last few years. However it soon became apparent to me that this was probably one of the hardest subjects on which to write. There are no hard and fast rules, no two people are the same. It was however while I was writing this that I discovered Mindfulness, and while in theory it is a form of meditation, it's basic tenet fits beautifully into every form of relationship challenge.

Most of us go along through our lives on automatic pilot, unaware of how our actions and reactions impact not only on ourselves but on those around us also. We gradually fall into habitual patterns of behaviour, we have our public faces and our private faces and we have our relationship faces. These, like our reactions become so much a part of us that to a greater extent we don't even know they are there. Wouldn't it be interesting if we could see ourselves through others eyes. If you thought about it, would you actually like what you saw?

Do you hear how you have grown into speaking to your partner when they irritate you for the hundredth time with that little habit they have? Do you speak negatively to them more often than you speak positively? Do you treat friends and acquaintances better than you treat your life partner? Is the relationship evolving, or has it evolved into your ideal relationship or do you feel you are always having to stamp your foot to get the action or reaction you want? Did you realise that how you spoke influenced the result you got?

So perhaps being Mindful of what you say, why you say it and how you say something may just help you towards healing a battered relationship, or start you off on the right foot with a new relationship. What I actually learned about Mindfulness and relationships was that there were times when being Mindful enough to say nothing reaped the greatest rewards. At other times I have found that being aware of how I said something and my choice of words changed what I said from a demand into a request.

I have found that it is a great game and it is relatively easy to play. The main beneficiary is you. You can play this game in every area of your life but as relationships are sometimes one of the most challenging areas it is a great place to start. It only takes awareness and intention. Feeling like you are stuck in a rut with no choices is a truly frustrating place to be but knowing that you can improve any situation by changing your approach and your perspective can be liberating and motivating. So why wouldn't you want to be in a Mindful relationship with yourself and your chosen partner.

Foreword

I first met Leigh a few years ago – we were both students on a course for therapists.

From the start, it was clear she was head and shoulders above the rest of us. While we saw two or three clients a week in the new technique we were learning – she saw thirty. That alone would have been enough to make us hate her – but her amazing generosity (every single week she brought a big packet of the best, most delicious biscuits in!) and her personality made us love her instead. She's warm, funny, vital and generous. As I got to know her better I realised she had some powerful insights into a better way of living. In the areas of better sexual relationships, better eating and better living, you'll find her mindful approach clear, candid, and life-enhancing. She shares aspects of her own life: all she's learned is condensed into the books, yet with practical techniques that you too can follow. There's nothing glib: she admits her own mistakes, and what she's done to change. I am using some of her ideas in my own life now – and feel so much more alive. You can never have too much love…that's one view I share with Leigh. But first you have to love yourself. Leigh's books aren't just full of wisdom – they're easy to read and funny too. Mindful living isn't heavy or difficult. It will bring you so much joy. And you can get high on life! Read Leigh's books and give it a try. I'm proud to say I helped her a little bit in getting the words down… but the knowledge is all hers. She helped me on a personal journey to happiness – she'll help you too.

Diana Cambridge
www.dianacambridge.co.uk
diana@dianacambridge.co.uk

Dedicated to

the man in the purple shirt...

Thank you to

My kids
for being amazing.

My ex-husband
for being supportive - regardless.

My family
for their belief in me - even when I am madly impulsive.

My friend who is a boy
for helping me become more Mindful.

My men
for their patience with me.

Diana Cambridge
for her guidance.

Leila Coppock
for her inspiration.

My Pilates pupils
for making my classes a joy.

My clients and patients
for their support in a job that I love.

Anyone who has crossed my path
for sharing their lives with me.

Radio 2s Chris Evans
the best tonic for positivity ever.

Phil Fisher
for all his incredible work. For helping me make my dream an amazing reality.

Contents

1. My New Year's resolution

How to get what you want
Rediscovering your Mojo
Making Lust last
Do I believe in relationships?
SOS

My New Year's Resolution

'I am interested in the modern suggestion that you can have a combination of love and sex in a marriage - which no previous society has ever believed' Alain de Botton

Last year one of my resolutions was to have 6 lovers - I achieved it. You can't write about it if you haven't experienced it, right. I learned such a lot and it has changed me and my perspective. I suppose one of the reasons I did it was because I had ended my 26 year marriage and it would appear to be a normal reaction to this new found freedom. One either falls straight into a new relationship, wallows in a mass of self-pity or goes off the rails for a while. To a certain extent, mine was the latter, but I had a three year period of celibacy before my sexual flame was ignited.

The first three years after my separation I spent getting my life as I wanted it to be and mentally switched off my sexual radar. I didn't just want a relationship for the sake of it, I didn't want a rebound relationship after the end of my marriage and the end of my love affair. If you have seen the film 'Somethings gotta give' with Diane Keaton, you will know what I mean. Diane's character throws herself into all sorts of projects to get over firstly the end of her marriage and then the end of her love affair. For a while during this period I thought that I had perhaps lost all interest in sex.

This would have been ironic as lack of sex was the predominant reason for my marriage ending. I realise now that it was just that I avoided it both mentally and physically. So one day after a particularly stimulating and flirty conversation with a guy I rediscovered my mojo. I found my cheeky, teasing and flirtatious side. And being free and single and overflowing with mischief I embarked on my mission. I feel, having got married at 19, that I hadn't really had a grown up relationship so the idea of having a lover or two was new to me. How to go about it was even more of a challenge, but oh how I love a challenge.

'being a sex symbol has to do with an attitude, not looks. Most men think it's looks, most women know otherwise' Kathleen Turner

How to get what you want

'Love is an ice cream sundae, with all the marvellous coverings. Sex is the cherry on top' Jimmy Dean

To know what you want, you have to know who you are. Sex isn't the be all and end all of life. But it is such fun. The thrill of the chase, the anticipation, it's all as good as the arrival at your destination. The nicest thing about a sexual liaison is when it is enjoyed for its own sake. No ulterior motives, no end game. I think that is why I thoroughly enjoyed the year of my 6 lovers. I wasn't looking for a life partner. I was just satisfying my curiosity. With the love of my life, 3 years previous, I had mind-blowing sex. We were like soul mates. I had so enjoyed the games we played and now I wanted to play them with other men.

When you are bubbly and have an obvious zest for life, you become attractive regardless of what you look like. If you seem like you are having fun, then other people want a bit of the action. And the more fun you start having, the more fun you have. I haven't got where I am today without a few challenges. I haven't always got it right. But I haven't stopped trying, changing things that don't work and trying again. My lovers were all so different. I was almost a different person with each of them. It was a fascinating fantasy world where I could explore who I was, and who I wanted to be.

You have to have courage in this life. The courage to try new things. It is only by doing this that you can be free. I still have great relationships with all the guys and my ex-husband I just no longer feel the need to play those particular games. It was a phase, a phase I had to go through to get me to where I am today and to help me evolve. I have gained confidence, independence, wisdom and strangely enough - peace. I am still cheeky and playful but I no longer need a conquest, an end result. I just enjoy the positive interaction.

'Kissing - and I mean like yummy, smacking kissing - is the most delicious, most beautiful and passionate thing that two people can do, bar none. Better than sex, hands down' Drew Barrymore

Rediscovering your Mojo

> *'Sex is always about emotions. Good sex is about free emotions; bad sex is about blocked emotions' Deepak Chopra*

When was the last time you felt really horny or lustful. Don't you remember what a wonderful NORMAL feeling it was. How it made you sparkle and glow. It made you feel alive and naughty. What is wrong with that? Just because you are grown up, doesn't mean you can't be playful. A client of mine, in her 70s, started seeing a guy after many years of widowhood. She didn't even have to tell me she had met someone, she just bounced and sparkled and blushed. She looked 20 years younger. I have had sex with really lean mean fit guys and if I let my hang ups about my stretch marks and saggy bits get in the way then neither of us would have had the fun we had. Whatever you do, do it 100%, make it fun.

Wouldn't you like that sense of wellbeing every day? It makes you tingle, it puts colour in your cheeks and it gets you noticed. If you have no-one to dress up for then do it for yourself, then you soon will have someone to dress up for. Some of my most romantic Valentines dinners have been by myself, for myself. I treat myself like I would treat a special someone. It really does make a difference to how you feel. If you have a partner you think you have fallen out of love with, then why are you still there. Have sex with them anyway, with your eyes closed and go with your senses. Think of it as a cheap workout, its cardiovascular, tightens your stomach and your pelvic floor!

Be in the moment, feel it, let go of all negativity and resentment, for yourself not for them. Just have the best light-hearted fun, for yourself. Give the best performance of your life, for you. You will blow their socks off and gain confidence at the same time. Don't look for feedback, who cares what they think? If it made you feel good, relaxed and alive then that's all that matters. Anything else is a bonus. Libido is normal. Lack of libido is not. If you have lost yours, want it back and playing around isn't doing it then see your doctor, try acupuncture or even hypnotherapy. Where there is a will, there is a way!

'I need sex for a clear complexion, but I would rather do it for love' Joan Crawford

Making lust last

'I know it sounds corny, but I do think beauty and sexiness come from within' Rachel Stevens

I think there is nothing nicer than having been out for the evening or the day with your partner and then going to bed with them and making out. Or you acknowledge that you are both whacked, have a snuggle and then drift off into companionable sleep. When you wake, you reach out for each other, drowsily reconnect, touch turning into caress, a quick nip to the loo! Warm bodies, heated sex. I love morning sex. Waking up my man in a very erotic way, there aren't many men who reject that wake up call!

As you may have guessed by now, I am a very physical person. I have had a very healthy interest in the opposite sex from an early age. This hasn't diminished with time. I am happy with sex or snuggles or any form of intimacy every day. Sadly my husband couldn't reflect my enthusiasm, partly due to his stressful work-life and partly due to our needs not matching. Still, sex, lust and mischief are a state of mind. I am not one to go down (so to speak!) without a fight so I was determined to make lust last. When all else failed I had been known to stand at the bottom of the marital bed and stamp my foot as I asked for more sex. It made me angry, frustrated, rejected and unhappy.

Lust and intimacy aren't necessarily just about the physical act of sex. Having a really nice time together, doing things together, being together, creating memories. Lust, desire grow out of shared experiences. Liking each other. Feeling your heart expand at the sight or thought of another person. Those feelings overflowing into physical desire, a need for that connection. The best way for two people to express their feelings for each other. A totally natural and normal extension of a relationship. And such fun. The silly thing is, it take very little to please most men. Sex once a week or once a month would keep a lot of men very happy. It is the prospect of never having sex ever again that saddens many.

'My boyfriend and I live together, which means we don't have sex - ever. Now the milk is free, we have both become lactose intolerant' Margaret Cho

Do I believe in relationships?

> *'Women need a reason to have sex. Men just need a place' Billy Crystal*

Before my 6 lovers I had only two proper sexual partners. I had no idea about the variety of sexual preferences or the different chemistry that can happen between two people. We all seem to crave a relationship, to have a special someone or more importantly, to be a special someone. We are bombarded with media images of romance and everlasting love. So much so that if you are alone, you feel abnormal. Everywhere you look there are couples. Blissfully happy, together.

But are they really? Are they all living a life of love and harmony? I am so grateful for all the experiences I have had to date, and all the men who have passed through my life. While they were all great guys I never felt the need to commit to anyone of them completely. I had no desire to move in with one, or have them move in with me. I love living on my own. It gives me time and space to be myself, because no matter how much I like being with someone, sometimes it is just nice to have your own space. Where you can find peace, have no-one to please or interact with, where you can fill yourself up before facing the world again.

I believe that is why many relationships are faltering. Living on top of each other, being sociable when you have nothing to give, having to compromise against your nature and sometimes losing who you are. All things that contribute to an accumulation of resentment and frustration that often overflows over trivial issues. These issues would not arise if we only interacted when we had the capacity to do so. When I was seeing my guys, I was always genuinely pleased to see them because I had had time for myself in the interim. Being sick of the sight of each other, and being together because you feel you have no choice will never lead to a harmonious relationship.

'They say marriages are made in Heaven. But so is thunder and lightning' Clint Eastwood

Mindful Relationships

Give yourself a chance to find out who you are by spending time alone.

Get pleasure out of your own company instead of always looking to others for it.

Great sex starts in your head

Feeling sexy isn't about finding a mate. It's about having a healthy liking for yourself.

Internal sunshine is the most attractive quality. Find out what excites you about life and do it - often

Look at all the beautiful sexy lingerie online; it will make you want to be playful.

Personal dissatisfaction will overshadow every area of your life. Be who you want to be.
You won't discover who this is if you stay in the life you are in without stepping outside your comfort zone.

Don't accept your lack of interest in the physical side of your relationship as just your age or normal. If you want a sexual or intimate relationship, find out how to get it.

Realise that everything that is said or done is judged and coloured from your own perspective

2. My marriage

It takes two...
Marriage vows
When the rot sets in...
Unhappily ever after
SOS

'I love my husband but...'

My Marriage

> *'Being a husband is a whole-time job. That is why so many husbands fail. They cannot give their entire attention to it'*
> *Arnold Bennett.*

I was 18 when I met my husband. I got a job in the local pub in the evening to meet people. He was a regular who seemed very cool as he was 6 years older than me. We started going out and had a nice time. We had quite good, if ordinary sex... whatever that is. I guess when you are young nice sex is good enough. It was quite basic and I don't think I orgasmed in the beginning which wasn't really an issue for me. I think I was quite naive then and was quite happy with petting and penetration.

I remember thinking, not long after we moved into our first home, that he wasn't as interested in sex as I was. But I didn't dwell on it as we were good friends and had other things to think about and do. On reflection I think that a mediocre sex life is probably okay (for me anyway) if other areas of your relationship are good. It is only when disappointments accumulated, resentments set in that it becomes an issue. My ex-husband is very generous, hard-working and would do anything for you - build anything, never say no and was very supportive. These are great traits in a friend or brother, and may well be all some women want from the man they are in a relationship with.

Sadly it was not my idea of a close, warm and intimate relationship. I need warmth, hand holding, connection. I realise now that I am older and wiser that not everyone is capable of this type of display of their feelings. Whatever you focus on, whatever becomes the focus of your attention is what will end up being the only thing you see. I got so hooked up on what he didn't do, didn't say that I took for granted what was good. There was actually more good than bad. A lot of men consider working hard, providing for their family as their expression of love and devotion.

'Women desire six things: they want their husbands to be brave, wise, rich, generous, obedient to their wife, and lively in bed' Geoffrey Chaucer

It takes two

'Sex is hardly ever just about sex' Shirley Maclaine

So I admit, half the blame is mine. If I had reacted differently, then perhaps my husband would have felt inspired to reciprocate in some of the ways that met my expectations of a close relationship. I remember once, telling him about a particular fantasy of mine. I had read that this may be a way of changing or improving ones sex life. However after this disclosure, he never once attempted to make that fantasy a reality. (It wasn't anything perverse!) When we were separating he said he remembered what my fantasy was, but never felt compelled to act upon it.

What I have learned over the last few years is that you need to be the person you want to have a relationship with. Instead of waiting for them to hold your hand, take theirs. Instead of waiting for a goodnight kiss. Give it. A client of mine in her 60s and on her third husband, always leaps on her husband when she gets into bed and gives him a playful big hug and kiss. She says that on the rare occasion that she doesn't, he makes no attempt to reciprocate. 'Its just the way he is'. But he is her constant support and chauffeur and she is content with their roles. She tried an experiment whereby, for a week she didn't leap on him. After a while he asked her if anything was wrong.

I always made the effort with my marriage. Never once did I refuse sex, stay in bed while he got up and went to work - I made coffee, packed lunches, made sure he always had tobacco and Southern Comfort. On the morning of our 25th wedding anniversary I gave him a card and present. His response was that he thought it was next week. Next week, being Valentine's Day, I didn't get a card or a present either. What I didn't realise at the time was that perhaps his reaction to our personal relationship was in response to my attitude to him. I just couldn't see it because I was so fuelled by my own rage at the injustice.

'Love is an irresistible desire to be irresistibly desired' Robert Frost

Marriage vows

> *'The gift of marriage brings husband and wife together in the delight and tenderness of sexual union and joyful commitment to the end of their lives' Church of England Marriage Service*

Most of us enter into a relationship or marriage with unspoken and subconscious expectations of how it will be. So what happens if one or other of the parties begin to renege on their part of the bargain? Even if a couple is not married, the same emotional criteria apply. We expect our partners to live up to their part of the written (marriage vows) or unwritten rules of engagement. If these needs are constantly ignored does their partner, therefore have the right to have these needs met elsewhere?

It wasn't until I was researching this book that I read the marriage service. It was the first time I had heard it since I got married 33 years ago. I don't even remember any of it or what it implied. Although many of the points mentioned in the vows are taken as read when you are madly in love and setting out on a life together, they aren't issues. It is only later when the relationship starts to falter, that you start to think, hang on a minute, this isn't what I signed up for. I like the intimacy, the sex, the warmth, the friendliness, the connection. I didn't sign up for indifference, neglect, nagging or criticism.

Many men I know are happy to live with their wives, support them, go on holidays and be a part of a family, but their sexual desires lie elsewhere. This is particularly the case if the physical side of the relationship has declined or if the needs of one partner is greater than the other. Many of us crave a healthy loving relationship. I feel now is the time to re-negotiate the marriage vows to read ' love, honour and respect providing we are meeting each other's needs or are at least willing to try. And that we are able to end the relationship if it is no longer working for us.

'We can welcome marriage as an institution that endures from day to day without seeming to pay too much mind to what its members are feeling' Alain de Botton - author of How to get more sex.

When the rot sets in

'When men and women agree, it is only in their conclusions; their reasons are always different' George Santayna

I know from personal experience that over time, the lime scale of your partners' small misdemeanours and neglect takes its toll. It is not just one thing that kills your love and desire over the years. You start to build up a wall around your heart. Sometimes you take it down when things are going well and you begin to trust and believe that you are with the right life partner and then all of a sudden - wham - another let down or the same disappointment that grows every time it is experienced. Your partner doesn't do what they said they would, they don't bother about your birthday or anniversary. They just don't seem to care. You are not on the same wavelength.

You construct the odd fragile truce. Patch it up, vow to try better at being the loving partner. But life takes over and that old default setting that has evolved over the years in the dynamics of your relationship switches back on. I had a Welsh wooden love spoon which came to represent my relationship with my husband. It would fall off the wall and break, so I would stick it back together and put it back up. It was fragile but it managed to stay up for a while. Then down it would come again and break and so on....... Eventually I left it on the windowsill so that it would fall and break again. One day I put it in the bin, having tired of seeing it battered and patched up. Subsequently my marriage ended.

You hope that patching it up, gluing it back together will be sufficient to hold it together because it is so much easier than the upheaval of throwing in the towel. As my marriage waned, I remember taking my husband away to a hotel. Packing sexy lingerie, sex toys, bondage props and hoping for an injection of lust and play... I set the scene... told my husband what we were going to do to each other... his response... "I'll just have a coffee and a fag first". I battled on regardless. But you can lead a horse to water, you can't make it drink. What was the problem... sexual incompatibility... he's just not into you anymore... boredom. Who knows. When asked now, my ex-husband does not know why he acted as he did then. But rejection, not being desired, no matter how old you are, takes its toll.

'I consider sex a misdemeanour - the more I miss, de meaner I get' Mae West

Unhappily ever after

'When you hold a grudge, you want someone else's sorrow to reflect your level of hurt but the two rarely meet' Steve Maraboli

One survey asked terminally ill patients if they had any regrets - 70% said being married to the wrong person. I know from the many conversations I have had with people that many would have cut and run if it didn't cause such terrible repercussions and dire consequences, not forgetting poverty! People don't want to intentionally hurt a person with whom they have spent many years. Had children and a history with. But at what cost? More people over 60 are now separating because one or other of them has decided that this isn't the person they want to grow old with. Some people may call it selfish - but what is selfish about desiring a life, your only life to be happy and good for you.

I know of several people who feel they should have jumped ship 20 years ago. They now feel like it is too late. Their only hope is that their partner will die before them. Now before you tut or raise an eyebrow at this, it's not that they are wishing them dead. They are used to having them around. They are just hoping for some peace and space of their own. Some time when their hackles don't constantly rise because he or she has left the cup there again, or not done the thing they were asked to do five times, or had to repeat some thing because their partner is going deaf and won't wear a hearing aid. I know a guy in his 70s who for many yeas now has been emotionally abusive and very uncomplimentary about his wife and yet is very affronted because she will no longer have sex with him. I suggested he be kinder to her - he couldn't bring himself to do it. The resentment was too deep on both sides.

This guy's wife has put up a big brick wall around her heart. As I did. Which is a shame because she is a lovely warm giving person - just not to the thoughtless bully who has hurt her and sapped her of her self-confidence. Why on earth would she want to give herself to him. So the cycle will continue. Both fearful of being alone, or being lonely so they stay with the devil they know. They feel they can't change their situation or the dynamics of the relationship they are in. They feel helpless and hopeless so they often strike out verbally adding more fuel to the bonfire of their marriage. I realise that this could have been me in 20 years time if I hadn't had the courage to go.

'Sometimes I wonder if men and women really suit each other. Perhaps they should live next door and just visit now and then' Katharine Hepburn

Mindful Relationships

Always speak to your partner with respect, as you would a valued friend.

If you have an issue about something, choose your moment. Not when you or they are tired or pushed for time. Ask when would be a good time to discuss it, make a date.

Try saying 'please remember' rather than 'don't forget'. Make it a request rather than a demand or order.

Try to keep your grievances to yourself rather than share them with the world and his wife. After all you have chosen to be with this 'terrible' person, so what does it say about you.?

Don't be reactionary. Remove yourself from any conflict and only reconnect when you are feeling calm and peaceful.

Remember we don't all show our love and affection in the same way. It doesn't make it wrong, just different. Switch your radar to the things your partner does to show they care.

You have a choice. You can choose to act positively or negatively. What you choose to say and do dictates how your relationship will be.

Don't accept being okay in your relationship, you only have one life. You deserve more.

If you have to work so hard at it that it is exhausting you, you need to decide if all that effort is giving you the return you want. It is very likely that it is not. This will lead to a build-up of anger, resentment and frustration.

Work on yourself, your life, it is not one dimensional; you are not just a person in a relationship.

'I love my husband - but'

I do love my husband but it isn't a romantic love anymore. I am very fond of him, he is a good man and sometimes I feel guilty because I don't feel the way I used to about him. We are more like friends now, companions. We do things together, golf, go on holidays and it's comfortable. But I am not sure I want to feel just comfortable for the rest of my life. I don't think I want anyone else. I would just like life to be less samey, less predictable.

You know, sometimes I wake up in the morning and I look over at him and think oh no not another day with you. Listening to him making the same comments, telling the same stories, moaning about the same things. I think it is easier when you are not retired because you don't see as much of each other. You are busy with your work, housework and everything else. I wish I didn't feel like this but how do you change it. I feel that I am too old to leave and really there is no real reason to leave, boredom probably isn't grounds for divorce!

I envy some of my friends who are on their second or third husbands, so they are still in their honeymoon periods. Everything is a new adventure. They have re- invented their lives, going new places, seeing new things. Still finding out about each other, still enjoying each other's company. I am sure I still love my husband but I'm not in love with him. There is no passion or lust. He is like a comfortable pair of slippers but sometimes I feel like I want high red stilettos!
Alison – Blandford, Dorset

3. The love affair

The affair
The others
The boyfriend
SOS

'I learned one thing from marriage... It's impossible'

The love affair

'Don't cry because it's over. Smile because it happened' Dr Seuss

When I met the love of my life, he was as desperate for love and affection as I was. When he realised his feelings for me were growing, he stayed away for six months. He was married and a very good man. However, as with me, the craving for physical human connection was too great. Sometimes just seeing someone who you are falling in love or lust with is enough, and we were just happy with that for quite a while. Then there was the kiss on the cheek, then just before Christmas - a kiss on the lips. My lips tingled for hours and I didn't sleep that night.

At this stage I had been married 25 years and he had an unblemished 35 years under his belt. Neither of us, by choice, would have been unfaithful. It was something we both struggled with endlessly. The first time we got intimate was like all our dreams had come true. He was so warm, he exuded warmth and I was unreserved, open and giving. As he left he touched my cheek and I fell truly, madly, deeply. There was a twist to this lovely tale though. He had erectile dysfunction. How desperate must he have been to even consider a relationship knowing he may not be able to perform.

I didn't care though. I would do anything in return for the warmth I received. I threw myself wholeheartedly into 'curing' him. Three months later, while away at a cottage, the most magical time of our lives, we achieved 'the orgasm'. I think this was one of the reasons our sex life was so incredible. We felt like soul mates. We made love, we had adventures. The earth truly moved. We fell asleep in each other's arms. We fed each other with all the things we didn't have with our respective spouses. It was a bitter sweet 20 months, we were always both torn. Alas it wasn't meant to be. With love we said goodbye. He said if he were ever free he would come and get me ......

'I have found the paradox, that if you love until it hurts, there can be no more hurt, only more love' Mother Teresa

The affair

'Love is an irresistible desire to be irresistibly desired' Robert Frost

So having resolutely vowed never to get involved with a married man ever again, I found myself having an affair with one. The difference is, that it wasn't love. He was someone who I saw quite often. He had always been flirtatious and friendly and while we had had banter I never felt the need or desire to take it any further. However it was my year of 6 lovers so one fateful day, I dressed with care. He said just the right thing, the green light. The next time we met, my plans laid ... and we ended up in bed. We were both absolutely blown away; we just clicked physically and mentally.

It was fun because I wasn't looking for a relationship, just someone to play with. And boy was he just the man for the job! Thus began a myriad of eloquent emails. His verbal skills matched his sexual prowess. When you are with someone who is on your wavelength then the interaction is incredible. The downside is that it makes you greedy, addicted. He loved all my games and dressing up. The lovely thing about my amazing lovers was that neither was a gigalo. Neither had had more than two or three sexual partners but the right person inspires you.

While I had strong feelings for him, why wouldn't you have a great liking for someone you were having a fabulous time with, in no way did I want or need him for life. It was just nice to be with another man who really appreciated my mischief and games and who was excited by me. Neither of us wanted any more than we had. We were both happy with our times together as it was. I would say that it takes a lot of effort and imagination to keep things as exciting as they were then. And so we had a passionate affair for six months then parted company as lovers, but remain respected and valued friends.

'A man is already halfway in love with any woman who listens to him' Brendan Francis

The others

> *'Sex without love is a meaningless experience, but as far as meaningless experiences go it is pretty damn good' Woody Allen*

The nice thing about these 'relationships' for want of a better word, was that I did not get wrung out emotionally by them. We could just take it or leave it but were always mindful and respectful of each other's needs at any given time. This didn't make me feel cheap as I had instigated or been complicit on each occasion. Uncomplicated sex has its place if you are a sexual person. It's almost like having someone to play squash with. You just appreciate having a good time, at that moment.

Two of the guys were very experienced lovers and I was quite nervous before I went to bed with them. After all I had very little experience, married since I was 19. Prior to that I had previously only had a couple of pubescent relationships. So experienced I was not. But enthusiastic, energetic and imaginative I was. I think to be a good lover one has to be mindful of the other person's rhythms. It's almost like dancing, you have to move in time, be in tune. And basically, if you are a willing partner, most men are easily pleased!

Sometimes it doesn't work moving from friendship to lovers, it can become emotional. Most of my lovers have gone from friendship to lovers and then back to friendship. Men like uncomplicated relationships, most of them can't cope with emotional outbursts and neediness. They are great to have discussions with about life, love and stuff. So for a year I had fun, I learned more about men and became more tolerant and understanding. It was great to have some fun and then go home, back to my life and my freedom.

'Sex without love is merely healthy exercise' Robert A. Heinlein.

The boyfriend

'Love is when you meet someone who tells you something new about yourself' Andre Breton

It was December in the year of my 6 lovers and I had only had 5 so I was cutting it fine. I had known my number 6 for six months. I thought he quite liked me by the way he kept making eyes at me but it was taking him time to build up the courage. So in the end I helped him. The joy of texting. So we started going out. He was looking for someone to do things with, have adventures with. I was looking for number 6 to complete my challenge. You never know when and where your biggest challenges and lessons in life are going to come from...

It started off in a blaze of passion and lust, three times a day. I went back to his flat on the first night and stayed for three weeks. As I hadn't had a proper relationship other than with my husband, I threw myself into it wholeheartedly, as I do! He was quite blown away by my enthusiasm and energy and we ran before we could walk. It didn't really matter, it felt right at the time. There was so much I liked and loved about him. He has my energy and commitment. I felt peaceful with him.

He has been one of my greatest teachers to date. He has helped me to be a better person, more accepting and mindful. We like spending time together but we also enjoy our own space. Ours is a relationship unlike any I would have anticipated. I guess we are just friends with benefits. Since meeting him I have become more respectful and tolerant of people, acknowledging their right to be who they are. If it fits in with who I am and who I want to be then it will continue. And he is hot in bed!

'Never love anyone who treats you like you are ordinary' Oscar Wilde

Mindful Relationships

Don't judge. We are all making it up as we go along. Each of us is comfortable in a different place.

You have to be true to yourself, otherwise you will never find peace.

Accept who you are right now - nothing stays the same

Never feel guilty or apologise for who you are. You are being the best person you can be at any given time.

Not all love or love affairs are meant to be forever. Sometimes the people we meet are just stepping stones on the 'journey'.

Great sex with someone isn't necessarily a precursor to a full blown relationship.

You have to know when to give up. To live in failure, is to fail.

A good relationship should be the icing on the cake. Your life, the life you have made for yourself should be the cake.

There will be new, better, different experiences out there if you want them.

It may be a bit philosophical, but perhaps people do come into your life for a reason. Be grateful that your paths crossed, but acknowledge that it was just that. A crossing of paths, you may not have been destined to go in the same direction.

'I learned one thing from marriage ....it's impossible'

I was in my 60s when I married for the third time. I had been on my own for several years after my beloved second husband died. I felt like I needed a companion. Someone to go out with. When I met my third husband he was charming. We went places, planned holidays and it wasn't long before he stayed at my place and never went home. He was insistent that we got married, I wasn't bothered but did it to placate him. Sadly it wasn't long after the wedding that I realised I should have kept my distance.

I think I should sue him for false advertising. He is nothing like the man I first dated. He is reluctant to go to the far flung destinations we talked about, he is reluctant to socialise, he never wears the new clothes we shopped for together. He only likes plain food. He has no desire to move to the coast now when he was when we were dating. The list is endless. All we do now is snipe at each other. This is not how I envisaged ending my days. I wanted someone to have adventures with.

Several of my friends were so envious of me when I got the courage up to leave my first husband. Even now, many of them, trapped in a boring loveless relationship wish they had jumped ship earlier before it was 'too late'. I would recommend having a man friend to go out with occasionally but make sure we live separately so that the magic doesn't die as quickly as it seems to when you either move in together or get married. Carole - Hampstead

4. Great sex

The Bedroom
Setting the scene
Games
Great Relationships
SOS

Great Sex

'It was a woman's bedroom, actually a boudoir; and no man belonged in it except by invitation' Kathleen Winsor

When did the bedroom become the hub of all things sexual - the place where power and control take over? The gaping chasm of the relationship is reflected in the distance between you in the marital bed. I felt lonelier in my bed when my husband was there than I ever do sleeping alone. When my marriage of 26 years ended I spent the next five years sleeping on my own - I went to sleep happy and relaxed, I no longer slept like a dormouse curled up on one corner, my arms crossed over my heart.

Two of my best friends now sleep in separate rooms from their partners. Sleeping in a different room is often a comment on the state of a relationship. When I moved into the spare bedroom, my husband knew our marriage was over more than anything I had said on the subject. However I also know of people in good relationships who just crave a good undisturbed night's sleep, free from trips to the loo and snoring. Someone once said about not sleeping in the same room as her husband - 'you are confusing bed with sex'.

I know of many people who would love to have the courage to distance themselves from their bedroom politics. How many women stay up late hoping their husband is asleep when they go to bed? How many men rather than go to bed sexually frustrated, stay up watching television or surfing the internet? A physical relationship is normal, healthy and fun if you are with the right person. It may have died of boredom or got buried under a layer of responsibility and domesticity. It doesn't have to be quantity, but it sure can be quality.

'You can be childlike without being childish. A child always wants to have fun. Ask yourself, 'am I having fun?' Christopher Meloni.

The Bedroom

'Our life is what our thoughts make it' *Marcus Aurelius*

My bedroom is a lovely peaceful place with a black wrought iron four poster bed with white linen drapes. I have wooden blinds and voile curtains. I have lamps and candles in exotic holders to produce 'mood' lighting. There is a luxurious sensuous throw at the foot of the bed and in my box of tricks I have midnight blue satin sheets. I used to have wardrobe doors with curtained insets but have now changed them into mirrors, very useful ..... There is a deep pile rug next to the bed in which to sink my toes.

My four poster bed, is inspired by one of the most magical romantic weekends away I have ever had. There was a bed exactly like it there and held such wonderful memories for me that I had to recreate it (with the help of my Dads welding). I always go to bed happy. This lovely bed has led to some very sexy adventures from a Bedouin tent, a cave to a boat. Its frame is ideal for tying up all sorts of things in all sorts of ways and is perfect for the hanging of a sex swing! Even if you don't use your bed in a sexy way, nourish your inner child with a picnic in a den or in a tent.

You will never again feel the same about rice pudding and chocolate buttons eaten in a dark cave created by every throw in the house encasing your four poster in the middle of the day. The more magic you can incorporate into the ordinariness of your life, the less ordinary your life will be. I recently slept in a different bedroom in my house, with a different view, with the bed facing another direction. It felt like a holiday, particularly as it was at the weekend. It takes very little, other than the will and the enthusiasm to make your life special. So stop taking it for granted and make it into a place to soothe your soul and see how it permeates into other areas of your life, unless of course you can't be bothered...

'Life will always be, to a large extent, what we ourselves make it' *Samuel Smiles*

Setting the scene

'Life must be lived as play' Plato

Now supposing you are fortunate enough to be in a relationship where your mischievousness and sense of fun is either reciprocated or at least appreciated. Then this section is for you. It takes very little to change an atmosphere or create a mood setting. It takes a few props, and sometimes some courage and bravado... Men like variety, if they can't get variety in their women then variety in their sex life would come a close second!. This doesn't mean that every intimate moment has to be a performance. Just now and then. The lighter the mood the better. Life is too important to be taken seriously, and sex even more so.

I know from experience that anticipation is a potent aphrodisiac. Texts and emails are a great way to start the playfulness. And before you say it...... you are NEVER too old. One of my guys was 60 going on 21 and he threw himself into every game with as much enthusiasm as I did. I do a very good line in Scheherazade.... (the fictional wife of a sultan who, to save herself from being executed when he became bored with her, told enticing tales every night so that he would want to see her again ...)

Games don't have to involve a lot of time and rigmarole. Complete darkness, a blackout, eyes closed, hands guided, commands given .... Simple pleasures like melted chocolate licked from every part of the body. The lingering smell a sexy reminder for hours to come. One guy got so turned on simply by having his eyes closed and doing the whole tantric thing. One of my most erotic experiences came when sharing a bed picnic, when my lover kissed me and squirted his drink unexpectedly into my mouth .... I still find this an incredible turn on to this day.

'No man is a failure who is enjoying life' William Feather

Games

'Humanity has advanced, when it has advanced, not because it has been sober; responsible and cautious, but because it has been playful, rebellious and immature' Tom Robbins

Being blessed with a vivid and enthusiastic imagination is great. If you don't feel you have one, get inspiration from books. Where there is a will there is a way. One of my favourite games is the Bedouin tent as it has such an exotic tone to it. I took the voile drapes from my windows and pegged them to my bed, completely enclosing it. Coloured candles in glass jars or beaded containers were strewn around the room. I put grapes and Turkish delight on nice gold plates and wine in fancy red champagne flutes. I brought a harem costume but a sarong or even a tablecloth would suffice. Costumes aren't on for long...

The thing is, is to get as much fun out of the preparation as out of the main event. I actually recreated the Bedouin tent in the back garden with a gazebo on a hot summer's night with fiery torches at the entrance. That was so much fun to do. I get as much pleasure out of the planning and creating as I do the playing. When I made the cave, I gathered every throw and blanket, even duvet covers I could find and completely encased the bed frame so that no light could get in. My fur rug was the cave floor. Red fairy lights in one corner was the fire.

I got a cave girl outfit - again you can improvise ... cavemen and women wear shredded rags. My unwitting captive was taken prisoner and lead to my dark cave where I could use him for my pleasure ... he didn't put up much of a fight! It ended up being one of his favourite places and experiences - far from reality and the madding crowd. It's just good to have some relaxing time out, fooling around and knowing you care enough to make a bit of an effort. No pressure. Just fun.

We can all look relatively good in sexy underwear and seductive lighting is a life saver. Every man is different in what turns him on. A sexy confident and willing woman needs very little else. One of my men liked Superdry workout underwear. It doesn't matter what it is, if someone is lusting over you, you will feel sexy in a black bin bag. The love of my life said that to me once, that I would look sexy in a bin bag, so I did. I turned up in a black plastic bag with a belt, high heels and nothing else, he ripped it off me. Just be playful, it is irresistable.

'If you obey all the rules you miss all the fun' Katharine Hepburn

Great Relationships

> *'Extend to each person, no matter how trivial the contact, all the care and kindness and understanding and love that you can muster, and do it with no thought of any reward. Your life will never be the same again.' O Nandino - Author*

There are so many ingredients to a successful relationship - respect, like, love, tolerance, accepting, co-operation, compromise, fun, lust, warmth, thoughtfulness, friendship, commitment and loyalty to name but a few. You, no doubt, have your own ingredients. I think it depends on the individuals concerned as to how much of each ingredient they need to make it work. Being your own person, not losing your identity and growing together rather than apart.

My parents have a great relationship. They ALWAYS kiss hello, goodbye and goodnight. They have never not bothered with Christmas presents, birthdays, valentines or anniversaries. Their cards always have lovely words and are meant. I always admire people who do things like date nights, book their birthdays off to do things together, have little routines or rituals of togetherness and perpetually make the effort to stay connected to their partners. One of my friends has been with her husband 20 years and they still have sexy nights in. Every other Friday they take turns in organising their date night.

I am well aware that what constitutes a good relationship for one couple is not necessarily what would work for another. You know when you are in a great relationship when it gets better, when it and you grow. When your liking for each other increases and you love flourishes. When you look forward to seeing them. When you do little things, make small gestures and are consistently considerate and thoughtful. When you say thank you or show appreciation for even the smallest things and never feel taken for granted. One lady I know, who after being married 40 years still had butterflies in her stomach when she heard her husband coming up the drive.

'I want to be in a relationship where you telling me you love me is just a ceremonious validation of what you already show me' Steve Maraboli

Mindful Relationships

Great sex starts in your head

Look at all the beautiful sexy lingerie online. It will inspire you and make you feel mischievous.

Are you doing fun couple type things now and then or has life sunk into a domestic rut?

Try going back to basics - just a good night hug and kiss, just a morning snuggle until the anticipation becomes unbearable then ....

If you and your partner have lost your connection and you want to regain it, don't go for big gestures and obvious moves. Start off with small things like changing how and what you say and do before going to sleep. Try for one week just touching their cheek or shoulder when saying goodnight.

IF you want to make changes of any esthstetic nature, do it for yourself. You may get a sexy response from your other half.

Don't take anything too seriously. Anything you do for the good of your relationship can only be positive..... do nothing and nothing will change.

If you want a great relationship - be a great part of it. Be the change you want to see in your relationship.

If you want your relationship to be a lifelong love affair, be a contributing factor. Lead by example rather than demand the attention.

"Couples who play together, stay together'. When was the last time you fooled around, had a pillow fight, a water fight, tickled, teased, put your cold hands up their tee shirt? Life is too important to be taken seriously. We do all have an inner child.

If you want to try out some mischief, start small. Maybe a hidden note, an unexpected text with a hidden meaning or ended with ....

You are more likely to feel loving or peaceful if you have somewhere that is your sanctuary. Your life and home maybe chaotic so do yourself a favour and make your bedroom a clutter free sensual zone.

If your overtures are rejected, do something nice for yourself. Treat yourself the way you would like to be treated. Acting angrily to rejection isn't going to have the desired effect of a more loving relationship.

This is your life you are creating. You will never regret bothering ...... I don't

'Monogamy? isn't that another word for monotony?'

I have been married for over forty years and my husband and I are great friends. We have had, and still have many adventures. We have never taken each other or our relationship for granted. We ran a business together and were a great team. I don't think we have ever stopped considering each other or respecting each other. It most certainly has never been monotonous. I think monotony is a state of mind. If you cannot make life interesting with one person you will probably get bored after a while in another relationship.

It doesn't matter who you are with, it is about your attitude to the relationship and the person. My life is fun, I keep it interesting. I see my relationship with my husband as the icing on my cake, not the cake itself. We don't live in each other's pockets, we have separate interests. We spend time together because we want to not because we have to. Even after all this time we still leave each other little notes, saying I love you. The other day my husband had cut out the 'I love' off of a cereal packet and wrote 'you' and left it in my make up bag.

I leave him notes in his clean laundry. Life is too exciting and interesting to be boring. I believe couples who play together, stay together. I don't think there is any secret recipe to a happy relationship, but being good friends is a start. We both equally put effort into our marriage, because we want to not because we have to. Although everyone is different, I have never felt the need to be with anyone else. I have found everything I need in one man. Pamela – Andover, Hampshire

5. Fidelity

Why men stay
Old habits die hard
Economics
Double lives
SOS

'My double life'

Fidelity

> *'A long lasting marriage is built by two people who believe in and live by the solemn promise they made' Darlene Schacht*

In modern relationships, fidelity is thought of in terms of sexual monogamy. In western culture it implies adherence to marriage vows, 'forsaking all others'. The expectation of fidelity isn't a free gift. It, for want of a better word, should be earned or reciprocated. If a partner in a relationship isn't playing their part then it is unfair to expect the social rules to be adhered to. I think that living with someone, sharing a bed and a life demands/dictates, warrants a certain amount of connection and affection. If this is lacking, then the cohabitation that ensues has to be accepted and acceptable to both parties.

Fidelity isn't a right, to be expected in a marriage or a relationship when there is no reciprocation of physical intimacy, closeness or warmth. The fact that another human being is suppressing daily, his or her natural desire to feel a connection with another human being in the most intimate way can take its toll. And I don't necessarily mean just sex when I say intimacy. It can be anything from a kind word, a thoughtful gesture or even something as simple as a touch on the arm, shoulder or anything that implies connection.

Fidelity for many means loyalty to one person, physically and emotionally. When an affair is discovered, the first question for many is 'did you sleep together?', 'have you had sex'. We aspire to a relationship where we are the centre of another person's universe, it is a closeness and connection that is greatly sought after. But the crux of the matter is, if you are not putting the required energy and commitment into it, it will deteriorate. Most people don't want to have affairs or end a relationship, being unfaithful does not sit well with most. For many there is as much angst as there is pleasure. It is very hard to be faithful to someone who does not return your affections. It's like hitting a ball to someone and them never hitting it back.

'Fidelity is a gift, not a requirement' Lilli Palmer

Why men stay

'Success in marriage does not come merely through finding the right mate, but through being the right mate' Barnett R. Brickner

For many decent men, the hardest thing to do is leave the family home. Even if they have found the love of their lives, they are racked with guilt over not being the protector and provider of their families. A couple I know who are now in the 80s, married for 25 years, had an awful job untangling themselves from their spouses. He left and went back several times to try and make a go of it with his wife, not because he loved her, that had died many years before, but because of his sense of duty. His wife of the time had him back, not because she loved him but to make him suffer for his sins. He was made to sleep in the box room. The first time of leaving was the hardest and eventually he left permanently and has been blissfully married ever since.

Many of the men I have met who have had or are having affairs don't actually want to be unfaithful to their wives. For several reasons. Basically many of them do love their wives but they get to a stage where they need their egos boosting, or their confidence or morale raised. By middle age or beyond they may feel the need to reaffirm their masculinity and manhood after years of being treated indifferently by their wives. Several of my lovers, when showered with praise and admiration remarked that it was nice to be appreciated. I suppose they felt taken for granted when all most of us want is to be noticed and our efforts to be appreciated. Most of us are probably guilty of that.

Even when the pull of a new partner or love is great, the sense of responsibility and duty is equally as strong. So many men, and women for that matter, are torn between the two. I know of several people who have let go of the love of their life because they cannot bear the thought of their spouse coping on their own. They sacrifice their heart for their head. People who have affairs, on the whole, are not bad people. They don't intentionally set out to hurt anyone.

'Over time, any deception destroys intimacy, and without intimacy couples cannot have true and lasting love' Bonnie Eaker Weil

Old habits die hard

> *'Women leave their marriages when they can't take any more. Men leave when they find someone new' J. Courtney Sullivan*

Another reason men find it hard to leave is familiarity and habit. Change is scary; there are no guarantees that you are not going to jump from the frying pan into the fire. No guarantees that the gorgeous loving woman you are crazy about isn't going to turn into a frigid nag like their wife. They find it hard to imagine going home to a different house, having a different routine, and for all their faults, their wives know what they like and how they like it. They don't have to make quite as much effort as they do with a new vibrant enthusiastic partner who is keen to do new things and go new places with their new partner.

A young guy I have known for several years, was so unhappy in his marriage, but could not see a way out. He longed for his wife to give him some love and affection. Eventually he had a bit of a fling which made him feel better but also confirmed to him that he really did want to be loved and desired. It took him many years before he got up the courage to leave his very bad marriage and he was so much happier. However he still longed to be back in his family home, living his life with his wife. No matter how bad it was ..... it was familiar.

I was once told by a lady who had been married many years, that marriage was like a tepid bath, not comfortable but better than the coldness once you are out of it. It has been said that men live longer when they are married and women live longer when they are single. Marriage, for many men, is a constant, even in a bad marriage, they know where they are. They are not totally alone. My ex-lover was very fearful of ending up on his own, if his wife threw him out and I no longer wanted him, where would he be.

'You don't repair that relationship by sitting down and talking about trust and making promises. Actually what rebuilds it is living it and doing things differently - and I think that is what is going to make the difference' Patricia Hewitt

Economics

> *'Divorce is the one human tragedy that reduces everything to cash'*
> *Rita Mae Brown*

I read recently that many people are staying married or not leaving home at least, because of the cost of living alone. Imagine the scene, you have been married 20 or 30 years, you've been successful, you have a nice house, nice cars, good holidays. However it has all become a bit routine. You are comfortable with your spouse, but you are not really ready to settle down to comfortable. You still need some lust, passion and excitement, and another exotic holiday just doesn't quite do it. You do however, like not having to worry about money. You like the prestige of where you live, after all you have worked bloody hard for this lifestyle.

Then one day, out of the blue, you find yourself irresistibly attracted to someone. The flirting starts and is reciprocated. Your pulse quickens and you feel more alive than you have for many years. You start an affair. It is amazing. Beyond your wildest dreams. You never imagined you could be with someone who is so utterly on your wavelength, who is so into you and thinks you are the greatest lover ever. You want this at all costs, you get as much of it as you can and it still doesn't seem to be enough.

Very soon you find yourself mentally weighing up the cost of leaving your spouse and living happily ever after with your dream lover. On the mad passionate days, you think you can do it, it doesn't matter as long as you are together. On the more sane days, you break into a cold sweat when you realise you may have to live in an area that isn't as good as you are used to. What if you divorce settlement is less than half? You are too old to recoup your losses. You start to look more critically at your lover, trying to decide if they are worth the economic devastation. You become torn. Which one could you live without? The love of your life or your comfortable life with your comfortable wife.

'Divorce is probably as painful as death' William Shatner

Double lives

'The meeting of two personalities is like the contact of two chemical substances; if there is any reaction, both are transformed' C G Jung

It is amazing how easily one slips into a life of clandestine meetings and snatched moments. And how quickly one adapts to the when, where, how and why of an affair. It almost becomes a mini life, a parallel life run alongside your other life. Interestingly enough, if done well, the two don't have to overlap or encroach on each other. I however, never got used to being the other woman, I hated it intensely. I always felt that if there was no future in it then what was the point.

I think you have to be a certain type of person. One of my friends has been having an affair for over four years. She is amazing, undemanding and unflappable. She never questions him about his home life or wife but lives totally in the moments that they are together. They manage weekends away, go out to dinner and do things other than just going to bed. They are completely in love with each other and feel it is the best relationship either of them has ever had. There are two reasons they are not together permanently. They are wary that they may lose some of the magic if they were together 24-7. Then there are the economics, he doesn't want only half of what he has worked for.

Most people having affairs tend to fit their lovers into the little pockets of their lives that don't overlap with their married lives. A retired guy I know invented a consultancy job that allowed him the freedom to come and go more easily. He managed to see his lover nearly every day for two years. It became part of his routine. Many people feel guilty about the deceit but they either learn to live with it, push it to the back of their minds or find over time that the feeling diminishes. It takes a lot of effort in the beginning to cover tracks, but a lot of the time the relationship with the spouse has plateaued to such a level that their indifference blinds them. People who have affairs are usually meticulous about keeping things at home exactly the same. Making sure that nothing in their routine changes.

'The moment we decide to throw more energy into fighting for our mate than with him, the crack of a fist on the enemy's jaw splits the ears of angels' *Beth Moore*

Mindful Relationships

Apportioning blame in any situation won't solve it. Accept the situation as it is/was and move forward from it.

Reliving, remembering and recycling the past only keeps it alive. It definitely is a case of least said soonest mended. But only if you can do this without internalising and letting the issue fester.

From silence comes wisdom. If you feel the urge to say something negative, accusatory or hurtful either go somewhere alone and say it to yourself, write it down and burn it, or write the text and then delete it, never send it. It will achieve nothing.

None of us are perfect. Remember daily all the good and positive things of the relationship and your life together.

Remember your marriage vows. Have you really kept your end of the bargain. An affair is only one way of failing in a marriage.

The fewer people you discuss your 'situation' with the less energy you will give it. Even if the people you are confiding in agree with you, it won't make you feel any better in the long term. It won't change what has happened. You have to change how you feel inside. Feel the anger and hurt but don't cling to it for your own sake.

Unresolved, unreleased negative emotions can lead to illness - why choose to make yourself ill.

If you really want to spend the rest of your life with this person, make today the first day of the rest of your live as if nothing went before.

Do you really want one part of your life to overshadow everything else, to be a spectre on your horizon for the rest of your life. This relationship is not the whole sum of your life and who you are.

If you have been unfaithful, don't spend the rest of your life feeling guilty and repentant. It's not healthy. You will lose yourself in the long run and end up in a worse position than before.

'My double life...'

I didn't set out to have this double life, I don't think anyone does. I thought I was just going to have a bit of fun, some uncomplicated sex with a very sexy woman. I do love my wife but you know what it's like ..... You begin to feel taken for granted, nothing you do is right and you feel that your sexual overtures are tolerated rather than desired. You end up feeling less than a man. My sex life with my wife had dried up almost completely and I stopped feeling I could bother her to satisfy my needs.

So when my flirty banter began to be reciprocated my imagination went into overdrive. I felt alive again for the first time in a very long time and the anticipation was intoxicating. Well we fell head over heels in love and lust the very first time we had sex. Neither of us had ever experienced such a connection before. It was mindblowing. We saw each other every day, texted all the time. We both wanted more but I just couldn't hurt my poor wife. She was a good girl, had been a good wife. I just loved this feeling of being alive, wanted, lusted after.

So four years on I have got used to living two parallel lives. I try not to lie too much about where I am. I find it much easier to be where I say I am, just not with whom. I don't miss any opportunity to have a night away working. I always feel torn between my responsibilities and my heart. I don't want to hurt anyone. I never anticipated feeling like this about someone who is in essence the love of my life. On one hand I feel I am not giving my all to anyone but on the other hand I fear that if I leave my wife to be with my lover it may stop being so magical. So until something changes I will carry on like this...... Paul - Brighton

6. What's love got to do with it

Fragile Truces
Making it work
When to throw in the towel
SOS

'My marriage is great... this is how it works...'

Men and women - we are different

'Sometimes I wonder if men and women really suit each other. Perhaps they should live next door and just visit now and then'
Katharine Hepburn

I have had many conversations with both men and women about sex, love and marriage and there have been many books written on the subject i.e. Men are from Mars, Women are from Venus. Men and women really do differ in how they think and feel about relationships. A man once told me 'men give love for sex and women give sex for love'. In Men are from Mars, John Gray says that ' without the awareness that we are supposed to be different, men and women are at odds with each other. We usually become angry or frustrated because we have forgotten this important truth'.

Many of the women I have spoken to, whether married or with partners, say very similar things. That their 'other half' doesn't do this, does that wrong, even after years of 'training' they still aren't giving flowers when they should, remembering to put the toilet seat down, paying compliments. So what happens is this lime scale of resentment sets in and the sexual/physical side of the relationship falters. Why? Perhaps because women need to be wooed and most men don't associate their behaviour with regard to their partners as relevant to having sex with them.

I propose that if your man finds it hard to do something even after being asked many times, then it is not in his nature to do so. I wish I had learned this when I was married. I learned this from my last boyfriend, perhaps my greatest teacher to date. I realised that some things just weren't important to him and so I began to overlook them, shrug them off, accept him totally as he was. I have to admit it was extremely hard, it wasn't my natural default setting. I had to realise it wasn't a personal slight against me, the things that could have bugged me just weren't on his radar. Acknowledge and respect differences. If not, then these differences of perspective will become festering wounds which will infect the rest of your relationship.

'When men and women agree, it is only in their conclusions; their reasons are always different' George Santayana

What's love got to do with it

'Sex without love is merely healthy exercise' *Robert A. Heinlem*

A loving relationship is one of our greatest desires and one of our greatest tests. Should we be making ground rules from the onset? Should we set out a charter of what our needs and expectations are? I shed a tear when I read Alain de Botton's book 'How to think more about sex' as he describes an all-encompassing marriage as a fairly new concept. I may just have been on the right track several years ago when I said I think one needs a spouse and a lover.

A recent lover said he had a love for me which he could not define. He did not know what love was. I think you can have sex without love, but you can't have a marriage without some kind of love. I liked all my lovers for various reasons. The sex was just a pleasant fun physical experience. The one I fell in love with was the one who began to meet other needs. Even then I realised that this was not necessarily grounds for or guarantee that we would live happily ever after.

My point is that sex doesn't have to grow into love. It is not a foregone conclusion. What gets forgotten sometimes in the throes of passion is that just because you are compatible in bed does not necessarily make grounds for a lifelong relationship. It is not personal, it is biological. No wonder there are so many unhappy depressed people out there. They live in the cage of marriage and live off the crumbs doled out by another, another who is meant to be the love of their life but who often treats them with at best indifference, and at worst mental cruelty.

Everything in the world is about sex except sex. Sex is about power' Oscar Wilde

Fragile Truces

'Indifference and neglect often do much more damage that outright dislike' J K Rowling

Have you got into a pattern of reacting to your partner, then when it has all calmed down, you settle back into a fragile truce for a while. Only to have it flare up again. Why the fragile truce? And why the flare up in the first place? Did they do something that was really bad, against you personally? Or was it just that your radar has become permanently switched to looking for the merest slight? The toilet seat not being put down, the cups not put in the cupboard in the right order, or any one of a hundred petty irritations. My mother suggests that when you really love someone you either don't notice the silly little things, you don't let it bother you and you mostly certainly don't let the resentment accumulate.

Why do we choose to stay in a relationship with someone who is so irritating that we feel we have to constantly police their actions. I met a guy who was having an affair, when he told his wife he pointed out that she always criticised him and put him down - she replied - oh that's just me. But the thing is, it wasn't just her, it was his confidence and self esteem that was affected. How many times after a 'row' have you both sat down and one of you has voiced your displeasure and the other has agreed to try harder. And so begins a fragile truce.

If after having discussed any issues that have become recurrent bugbears in your relationship and a resolution hasn't been found, then you have to decide if it is worth ignoring or divorcing over. A fragile truce is one that occurs when the cause of disharmony is not resolved. It will recur frequently. It will solve nothing. They don't have sufficient underpinning because both parties have to be in full agreement about the importance and gravity of the issue. Him leaving the toilet seat up constantly implies that it is not important to him, so you have to either let it go, or put it down yourself.

'I want to be in a relationship where you telling me you love me is just a ceremonious validation of what you already show me' Steve Maraboli

Making it work

> *'If you need something from somebody, always give that person a way to hand it to you' Sue Monk Kidd*

In the blissful beginning of a relationship, one's radar is tuned to pick up all the wonderful rosy things about your partner, all the things they say and do to make you feel loved and wanted. They are considerate and thoughtful. Put the lid on the toothpaste; even if they don't you don't care. Gradually as time goes by, you see more of each other; you start to notice what they don't do so well, things that you would do differently. Before you know it your radar is picking up all their irritating ways. You start feeling irritated, belligerent and cheated that they aren't the perfect being you first thought.

None of us are perfect, we are all individuals. So how can you get over this? How can you go back to adoring them? Well you have to choose to ignore all the unimportant petty niggles and focus on the positive things about your partner and your relationship. When I suggest this to people, they are not impressed. Why should they make all the effort when it's not them that is at fault. Nothing changes, if nothing changes. If you want to save your relationship then you have to do things differently. React differently, or don't react at all.

I have learned that 'least said soonest mended' allows us to let go of so many petty irritations. Be mindful of what and how you say things. Most things people do that 'annoy' us are not on purpose, are not personal and so shouldn't be reacted to as such. A lady I know stopped reacting to what her husband said or did. She only acted with gratitude to anything he said or did. As a result he stopped reacting negatively to her and started to act in the way she desired. Only positive reinforcement will give positive results.

'A happy marriage doesn't mean you have a perfect spouse or a perfect marriage. It simply means you have chosen to look beyond the imperfections in both' Fawn Weaver

When to throw in the towel

'When you stop expecting people to be perfect, you can like them for who they are' Donald Miller

If the gulf between you has become too wide then no amount of bridge building will hold it together. It will keep crumbling. How hard should you try to put it right? A woman came to see me every couple of months. She would regularly say that she and her husband were going away for the weekend to talk about their relationship. They went somewhere nice and instead of just enjoying their surroundings and each other, they or rather she would talk about the relationship. She could not see it but she had talked it to death and nothing had improved.

Are you able to wake up tomorrow morning and let go of all past slights and hurts, see the person you profess to love and want to spend the rest of your life with, from a new perspective then you have nothing to worry about. If not, then perhaps you need to start making plans so that you can make an informed choice about where you are going with your life. One lady I know, married for 25 years, took five years of planning and saving before she left. It was then that she met the love of her life.

So what are you going to do? Settle for friendship, companionship. Forget any notion of sex and romance. Or ... take a deep breath and jump ship. What I found is that no matter how you put it, if the person you are with doesn't have it in them to love you like you need or want to be loved then you have to face the facts...... they never will. There are no guarantees that you will get your happy ever after elsewhere. But like me, you may find that being in no relationship is preferable to the daily gnawing dissatisfaction of an unsatisfactory marriage.

'Marriage - if you want something to last forever, you treat it differently. You shield it and protect it. You never abuse it. You don't expose it to the elements. You don't make it common or ordinary. If it ever becomes tarnished, you lovingly

polish it until it gleams like new. It becomes special because you have made it so, and it grows more beautiful and precious as time goes by.'

Mindful Relationships

Remember that you are a human being first, an individual second and in a relationship third. And so is your partner.

Approach each relationship challenge with kindness, patience and compassion - for yourself and your partner. Attack will only lead to a defensive response.

Lead by example. If there is something in your relationship which you would like to improve, don't talk about it, do it.

Give change a chance. If you have agreed on ways to improve a situation, give it time to settle in. Don't go for great big changes. Lay one foundation stone at a time.

Choose your battles. Choose when to remain silent. Leave negative things unsaid more often than voicing your grievances and see what happens.

Aim to be the person you would like to have a relationship with. Wouldn't it be nice if your partner was with you because they liked you rather than because they feel they have no other options?

Put yourself in the other persons shoes. How would you feel to be constantly nagged, criticized and made to feel inadequate.

Actions speak louder than words - if you have talked it to death - you won't be able to revive it the same way

If you can let go of the past hurts, stop dragging them up then you have a chance to move forward

This is your life you are talking about, this is serious stuff. Are the irritations really that bad or just superficial nonsense?
Have you started treating your partner worse than you would an acquaintance or friend?
Practise treating them with the same respect.

If both partners are willing, draw up a charter of what you would really like from this relationship and revisit and revise it often.

If you both really do love and value each other, then you will both be prepared to make the changes that will improve your relationship.

Try not to criticise and apportion blame. It takes two. You may think that none of it is your fault but there are none so blind as those who don't want to see - take it from me.

The break up of a relationship is never easy for either partners so be kind to each other. Or if they can't, you have to be.

Have you acted in a way that inspires your partner to treat you as you wish to be treated? Be mindful of your words, actions and body language.

It takes time and patience to stay or to go. Be patient with yourself and your partner.

'My marriage is great... this is how it works...'

I have been married for over 50 years and I can honestly say I have no regrets. I think I have been very lucky when I see how my peers are in their marriages. There is a lot of resentment and unhappiness that seems to have got worse over the years. I can see a great lack of respect and affection in most cases. Neither spouse has a good word to say about the other. There definitely is a lack of love. My husband and I love each other as much as we did in the early days if not more.

We have always kissed hello, goodbye and goodnight. I would say we have equal say in all decisions and I would never dream of talking negatively to him or about him. He still makes me laugh, brings me a cup of tea in bed and has never missed an anniversary, birthday or Christmas. I still get thoughtful presents from him. For my part I have never said no to sex and we still have many intimate moments even after he became impotent. Most importantly we still have fun and are friends.

The last half century has been amazing, we have had many adventures, and still enjoy each other's company. I feel very grateful to have found the right person to have shared my life with so far. I think one of the reasons it has worked so well is that we have never let things slip, never not bothered even when life got challenging we didn't let it affect 'us". We always treat each other as we would treat any other person but with extra love. Being friends and liking each other for who we are, is important - it requires effort. Shirley - Hammersmith

7. Life after marriage

What I have learned about myself
Moving on
What I have learned about relationships
And so...

Life after Marriage

> *'I believe that two people are connected at the heart, and it doesn't matter what you do, or who you are, or where you live; there are no boundaries or barriers if two people are destined to be together' Julia Roberts*

If you had told me six years ago that I would be in this position: single, living in a flat, running a successful business, being totally at peace with myself, I wouldn't have believed it. My life has changed beyond all recognition. Things I once only fantasized about I have now experienced. Back then I was overweight, angry, intolerant, critical and unhappy. I was stuck in a rut of reaction and ingratitude. I am now more me than I have ever been before and the possibilities are endless.

Having now experienced several amazing lovers, I have grown and evolved as a person. It wasn't necessarily that my amazing lovers were amazing in their own right; but when we were put together, the chemistry was incredible. I know there is something about newness and novelty, but neither I nor they had ever had such great sex before, not even on our wedding nights. Going to bed with a like minded person is a wonderful thing - when two people connect on such an intimate level it is magical. Both equally willing to please each other, revelling in the absolute mind- blowing experience of two people as one.

I did not really believe that it could exist, but I have honestly felt, first hand, the earth move. I have had such mind- blowing orgasms that I have not known what to do with myself. I feel this physicality, this thing called sex, is such a gift to the human race. Why then has it become taboo, been defiled, not exclusively by media and religion, but by ordinary human beings, sharing lives together. Who, had initially got together due to a physical attraction and need. A good relationship isn't solely based on sex unless that is what BOTH parties feel is a key ingredient. Being on the same wavelength, sharing mutual pleasures, and meeting some of each other's prerequisites of the relationship, are equally important.

'What we don't recognize is that holding onto resentment is like holding onto your breath. You'll soon start to suffocate' Deepak Chopra

What I have learned about myself

> *'You don't develop courage by being in your relationships every day. You develop it by surviving difficult times and challenging adversity' Epicurus*

When you marry young, or if some life experience or other takes you over, you can, in time, lose yourself. The real you can disappear under layer upon layer of negative thoughts and experiences. I would not be in the good place I am today if I had continued to act and react in my old ways. I have grown, developed and changed by trying to do things differently. Beit relationships with men, family, friends or acquaintances. No-one wants to give up a safe familiar life (even if it is unhappy) if there is no guarantee that the new one will be better.

Since I got divorced, I have started practising Mindfulness. I have learned not to let negative thoughts and feelings fester and linger. It is such a challenge in intimate relationships. Many of us don't realise that lifelong baggage contributes to us reacting the way we do. For my part, I realise some of my issues come from being the eldest child. My brother came along soon after and was always the blue eyed boy. Then when married, I was never a priority with my husband. So I guess I have always felt second best. But that was then and this is now.

I have learned that not being true to yourself doesn't wash after a while. The cracks eventually begin to show, and no matter how many times you cover them over, they will keep appearing. You really cannot not be who you inherently are. We all have basic needs which make us feel complete. Ideally you meet these needs yourself, but when you are in a relationship, no matter what type, there are some universal expectations of that interaction between two people that need to be met. So I have learned that no matter how much work you do on yourself, if there is no connection between you and the other person, it will affect you.

'Negative emotions are like unwelcome guests. Just because they show up on our doorsteps doesn't mean they have a right to stay' Deepak Chopra

Moving on

'Even if your heart ends up getting broken, the experience of being in love is worth it' Melchor Lim

We have two parts to our brains. The primitive, negative, over protective mother part and the intellectual rational part. I have to admit that for a greater period of my adult life, my primitive brain has been in control. Reacting rather than acting. Filling my head with repetitive negative thoughts and making myself deeply unhappy. And never more so than in relationships. My primitive brain, in order to protect me, kept me in a state of remembering things from the past, not letting it go, going over and over stuff 'he' or 'they' didn't do, what he said, what we did .....all past stuff and of no use whatsoever in the here and now.

I used to keep all the texts from the love of my life. I had three phones full and I would pour over them, becoming word perfect. I said to him once, that his words were like a buoy that kept me afloat. After time they stopped keeping afloat. So I began to sink. With my last boyfriend, again I started to collect texts. I had 1000 in the first month or so. I then realised what I was doing and so I deleted them after I had read and replied to them so that my primitive brain, my ego had less to feed on.

I am incredibly grateful for all that I have learned over the last six years and all the people who have helped me along the way. I still have a place in my heart for all the men who have passed through my life. I have chosen to keep my heart open after every heartbreak which I feel has increased my ability to love. I refuse to think or feel badly about anyone or any experience. If I had my time again I would do everything exactly the same so that I could learn the same lessons and end up right where I am right now.

'I want to be very close to someone I respect and admire and have somebody who feels the same way about me' Richard Bach

What I have learned about relationships

'My great hope is to laugh as much as I cry; to get my work done and try to love somebody and have the courage to accept the love in return' Maya Angelou

I am a person with incredible energy, enthusiasm and zest for life. I give more than 100% to whatever or whoever I chose to do. I think in the past I expected that back from the men in my life. I realise now that we all give and show love in different ways. Sometimes we are brainwashed by the media and Hollywood movies into subconsciously expecting fireworks and passion from those who purport to love us. When they don't we throw our toys out of the pram and collect so much negative evidence against them that it extinguishes our love.

A client of mine has two very attractive but single daughters who have yet to find a man who meets their expectations. Their father says they have watched too many romantic movies and life is just not like that. There is no knight in shining armour. Well I believe there are knights in shining armour but the armour is not necessarily that obvious. While I was looking and expecting gestures that reflected and matched my own, I was overlooking the things that my husband then boyfriend did as their own expression of love.

I show my love in one way, they show their love in another. You just have to learn to see the signs. It's not the big bunch of roses on Valentine' Day. It's the tiny gestures every day. I am so much better than I was at noticing the thoughtful ways of others. I used to be so intent on focussing on what they didn't do, that that was all I saw. My life and state of mind has become so much more peaceful now that I am not continuously spoiling for a fight, looking for reasons to criticise, or leaping immediately to defensive mode.

'So many people prefer to live in drama because it is comfortable. It's like someone staying in a bad marriage or relationship - it's actually easier to stay because they know what to expect every day, versus leaving and not knowing what to expect' Ellen DeGeneres

And so...

> *'Whatever relationships you have attracted in your life at this moment, are precisely the ones you need in your life at this moment. There is a hidden meaning behind all events, and this hidden meaning is serving your own evolution' Deepak Chopra*

I don't believe in avoiding life. I certainly won't be treading carefully through my life hoping to make it safely to death! The only way to grow, evolve and learn is to face life head on and dive in with true faith and conviction. I no longer let small grievances and annoyances fester and grow into all-consuming resentments that accumulate. I can let it all go and accept people (men) for who they are. Just because we are not on the same wavelength does not make either of us right or wrong, just at a different stage or place in our lives. And there may never be a time when we are on the same path. How nice though that our paths even crossed at all.

I am really looking forward to my next relationship with excited anticipation. I am looking forward to putting into practise all the things I have learned from the recent past. For something that is so inherently part of most of us .... being in a relationship ... some of us are ill-equipped or unprepared for how complicated the recipe for success is. However with all the right ingredients the results can be truly magical. Which is why we all hanker after that someone special to share our lives with.

I have evolved and don't want to play the same old games I played, getting the same results. I could have chosen to become bitter and twisted, I could have rebricked up my heart and played the 'poor me' card. I have chosen to keep my heart open and nurture it so it grows. And because I did, I have had so many wonderful experiences and will continue to have until I meet my perfect partner, he is coming, I know, I have been told...

'work like you don't need the money,
love like you have never been hurt,
dance like no-one is watching'

Mindful Relationships

You can't make people what they are not. Love them for who they are. If you are not on the same wavelength let go before the negativity takes over.

Don't accept being okay in your relationship, you only have one life, you deserve more.

If you have to work so hard at it that it is exhausting you. Stop. If you can't change the what, change the how.

Try not to keep making the same mistakes. If a relationship ends, give yourself some time, let the dust settle and see what comes out of the clearing.

Try not to waste time and energy going over what went wrong and why. Accept it and acknowledge what is good about now.

Talking, thinking and feeling negatively will harm no-one but you. Let it all go.

Don't be afraid to trust and try again. It won't be the same as last time, you are not the same person. The dynamics will be different.

Have a sense of excited anticipation about meeting someone new, not trepidation and fear otherwise you will be seeing it from the wrong perspective.

Rethink your expectations of a relationship. The relationship that works for you may not be stereotypical or the social norm. It doesn't matter.

Don't judge. We are all making it up as we go along. Each of us is comfortable in a different place.

Don't blame yourself or anyone else. Forgive everyone including yourself.

How to meditate

> *'Don't seek, don't search, don't ask, don't knock, don't demand - relax. If you relax, it comes, if you relax, it is there, if you relax you start vibrating with it' Osho*

When I started I tried with the breathing, focussing on my breath and I would find that even before the end of the first in and out breath my mind had wandered. I would drag it back and another thought would worm its way into my mind. Often when trying to clear my mind, it would feel like I had a bag of ferrets in my head as all my suppressed thoughts fought for supremacy. It took many times for me to get to a stage where I could keep my mind reasonably clear for more than two seconds. What I found worked for me was to start by feeling my face. I would close my eyes and feel the sensation of my eyebrows; if they were tense then I would stay with them until they were relaxed.

Then I would focus on my eyes and eye sockets. I found these were often more tense than my eyebrows and it took practise to mentally smooth them out. The last area was my jaw, when you relax your jaw, your neck, shoulders and whole body begins to melt. While I was doing this I was unable to think, then I could focus on my breathing. If I then found my mind starting to wander I would go back to feeling my face. Once I got better at this I began to feel wonderfully calm and peaceful in my body. I felt light with no tension. The sensation is so nice that I try for five minutes several times a day, it's like a tonic.

I find that Mindful meditation is like a sanctuary, a place to go if my day gets challenging or if some thought starts to dominate my mind. I don't even have to be sat somewhere to do this. Sometimes when I am driving and I need to calm my mind or clear my head I just focus on the sensations of my face and I find the source of my discourse dissolves, dilutes and disappears. I can honestly say I have many less thoughts than I used to and feel so much more peaceful. It does however take practise and consistency.

Books that have inspired me

The Power is Within you - *Louise Hay*

The Power of Now - *Elkhart tolle*

The Secret - *Rhonda Byrne*

The Book of Secrets - *Deepak Chopra*

The Law of Attraction - *Esther and Jerry hicks*

Willpower - R*oy F. Baumeister & John Tierney*

Sex is not compulsory - *Liz Hodgkinson*

The Way of the Warrior - *Dan Millman*

All of the books - *Paulo Coelho*

The Time Keeper - *Mitch Albom*

The Art of Happiness - *Dalai Lama*

Feel the Fear and do it anyway - *Susan Jeffries*

How to get from where you are to where you want to be - *Jack Canfield*

Having it all - *John Assaraf*

How to get what you want and want what you have - *John Gray*

Men are from Mars and Women are from Venus - *John Gray*

Sex Life - *Dr Pamela Stephenson-Connelly*

I can make you thin - *Paul McKenna*

The Game of Life and how to play it - *Florence Scovel Shinn*

How to think more about sex - *Alain de Botton*